M000188011

covenant

covenant

A Study for the
United Church of Christ

Jane Fisler Hoffman

Foreword by
Walter Brueggmann

UNITED
CHURCH
PRESS ®

United Church Press
700 Prospect Avenue
Cleveland, Ohio 44115-1100
unitedchurchpress.com

12 11 10 09 08   5 4 3 2 1

Library of Congress Cataloging-in-Publication Data

Hoffman, Jane Fisler, 1945-
    Covenant : a study for the United Church of Christ /
Jane Fisler Hoffman ; foreword by Walter Brueggemann.
        p. cm.
    Includes bibliographical references and index.
    ISBN-13: 978-0-8298-1794-2 (alk. paper)
    1. United Church of Christ—Doctrines. 2. Covenants—
Religious aspects—United Church of Christ. I. Title.
BX9886.H64 2008
231.7′6—dc22

                                        2008019283

Contents

Foreword

Jane Fisler Hoffman, whom I am proud to salute as a former student, has written a book that is timely, wise, and deeply grounded. The church in the United States — in its several forms — has largely lost its way. It seeks, in various modes, to order its life according to its moral passion — liberal or conservative — or according to its polity, which most often is a strategy for the management of power. But either ideology-tinged moral passion or polity, without a grounding in serious theological claims, cannot fully sustain a church body, or prevent it from becoming either an exclusionary sect or a powerless structure. The need to go deeper into theological rootage is an urgent work in the U.S. church, a task that Fisler Hoffman addresses in wise and knowing ways.

She takes up the biblical theme of "covenant," a theme written into the founding documents of the United Church of Christ, but a theme too easily preempted for lesser agendas. The theme of covenant pervades scripture. Seen in the ancient memories of Abraham and Sinai, it comes to visible form in "the cup of the new covenant." It affirms a rich possibility for rethinking and redescribing the nature of the church. Taken "horizontally," the covenant invites the church to a dialogic existence that eschews both authoritarianism and autonomy; against such pervasive temptations, covenant insists that we are members one of another, pledged to solidarity across ideological lines and prepared to live

7

in sustained engagement with each other in ways that impinge on and eventually transform all parties to the transaction. Taken in "vertical" form, covenant is the recognition that all members stand in accountability to a will and purpose beyond our own will and purpose. The God of that will and purpose is compassionately self-giving but, according to our tradition, also uncompromising in the assertion of holiness that transcends and overrides all of our preferred projects and ideologies. Covenant, as horizontal dialogic existence and as vertical demanding confrontation, yields a way of life that is always on the move, always summoned beyond our preferred way stations, always sustained when we move out beyond our comfort zone in faithful obedience. Fisler Hoffman knows of that theological reality and dares to assume and affirm it.

But Fisler Hoffman is not simply a responsible theological thinker — that itself no small matter. At the same time, she is a practical, experienced church leader and manager, fully aware of the quixotic ways of Christian community, fully informed about self-interest masquerading as moral passion, fully conversant with hard-nosed in-fighting that puts the body of the faithful in profound stress. In her practicality, she groans in anguish in the midst of a church that does not "get it." But she writes in hope, not having quit on the reality of the church that is her calling, her burden, and her true home.

I anticipate that Fisler Hoffman's study can serve as a wise, faithful, practical guide for church obedience in its concrete life. It is a guide that has no naiveté about the hard reality of church life and that has no innocence about the conflicted social context in which the church does its missional work. Her offer concerning covenant is a way of empowerment of church leadership, a way that asks church members to think again about the nature of our common life. Clearly anxiety is a debilitating condition for faithfulness in the church, for anxiety causes us to act in fearful ways, causes us to deceive ourselves about our vested interests, causes us to do destructive things to each other in the body. Covenant depends upon some freedom from anxiety. But it is also, itself, an antidote to anxiety, for serious covenant is emancipatory, a form of being heard and taken seriously, drawn into the serious action of the church in fidelity and freedom.

I am grateful for Fisler Hoffman's wise leadership. I anticipate that if the church — her own United Church of Christ and the church beyond her own denomination — will ponder in a serious way her exposition, it may find its way to revived energy that is congruent with the gospel we profess. While our society is deeply suspicious of the church with its long history of abusiveness and alienated from the church in its "business a usual," I have no doubt that many in our society are waiting for an available dialogic practice that shatters the fearful monologue of the modern world. Fisler Hoffman makes clear that the ancient term for such dialogic practice is "covenant." And we in the church with Jesus are invited always again to the newness of covenant.

Walter Brueggemann

Introduction

In an August 23, 2005, *Christian Century* article, Peter Marty cites the words of poet T. S. Eliot in the play *The Rock*, "What life have you if you have not life together?" From that provocative question, Marty's article unfolds his case for "community as a way of life" for the church in the United States during this millennium — an era when individualism (me, mine before all else) has become the true "American Idol." In such a time, the United Church of Christ (UCC) is exploring its identity and mission. There is among us a growing sense that the call of this unique denomination is to witness to the wide and inclusive love of Jesus Christ. But with this growing sense comes considerable and often divisive discussion about what all of that means among us. In those discussions and through all the upheavals and debates, a single word is often named as the "tie that binds" us together as community: *covenant.*

Though occasionally used in the secular world and recently by some corporations, "covenant" clearly is a "churchy" or religious word. And some who believe the modern church must discard all such traditional language to minister in a modern world are fueling a wave of resistance to the use of such words. In worship, there is surely a case for discarding some ancient language. There are some terms that could at least initially prevent new or seeking believers from understanding and participating in worship. For example, "doxology" is a word that would have no meaning to new Christians. But just as anyone new to a field of meaning must learn a new language, there are some essentials of non-everyday language that believing Christians need to learn and appropriate. This would enable them to grow and develop as persons of faith in mission with Christ. *Which* words are included in such a vocabulary for all Christians may be an ongoing subject of discussion. This study guide, however, is plainly claiming that "covenant" is one such word that needs to be claimed by those who are members of and particularly leaders in the United Church of Christ.

This resource is not intended to be a definitive scholarly treatise on all that covenant has meant and can mean in our faith tradition. There are many sources available to those who want to make that exploration, and some of these were consulted in preparation of this guide and are listed later. No, I have a much more modest goal, which will be named in a moment. But first a pause to explain: yes, I have intentionally stepped out of the traditional authorial custom of never using "I" in "expository" writing. "Covenant" is a relational term, and I hope this small resource can be an invitation and catalyst to conversations about covenant among people of our church who know themselves as being in relationship as part of the United Church of Christ. I am one such person and have written this in a somewhat conversational style as one of your conversational partners.

So it may be only fair for me to introduce myself briefly to you who may use this. Though raised largely in the Presbyterian Church, my husband and I, shortly after our marriage, did what is now known as "church shopping" and found ourselves welcomed by a lively United Church of Christ congregation in a St. Louis suburb.

That congregation mentored me, a former social worker and then full time mom, into adult faith, into positions of leadership (I was the youngest and first woman council president), and gave voice to my call into ordained ministry. Since graduation from Eden Theological Seminary, I served as an associate pastor and local church pastor (twelve years) and then was called into wider church ministry, first as an Association minister in Ohio and now as a Conference minister in Illinois. I have served in a variety of elected or appointed national UCC positions and am currently a member of the Executive Council. Each experience in each setting, as layperson and then ordained, has been a privilege and an opportunity to grow and share in the adventure of being part of this exhilarating, frustrating, faithful church known as the United Church of Christ.

Central to much of that adventure has been living in the mystery of how the UCC operates within our triple but often conflictive commitments to individual freedom, to congregational autonomy, and to covenantal life. A full, basic United Church of Christ "history and polity" background study may be a fruitful predecessor or successor to this discussion series. If that is not part of your plan, I recommend a review of the brief brochure *Who We Are and What We Believe* before launching into this exploration of covenant (available from UCC Resources, 1.800.537.3394).

Now for the specific purpose of this resource. In my now twenty-five years of ordained ministry in the United Church of Christ, I have led, participated in, and "sat through" uncountable opening moments of church council, committee, and ministry team meetings, as well as other gatherings of UCC folks. Too many have been three-minute nods to the possibility of God's involvement in what was to follow and some have even never gone that far. At times and in various seasons, some groups have committed themselves to spending twenty or thirty minutes in Bible study or other reflection. Other movements, evident in a few congregations, have attempted to make "worshipful work" of the entire meeting. But these are rare, as are meaningful resources for distinctively UCC gatherings. My small hope for this project is to offer a resource that can be used as part of the opening of gatherings of UCC local church councils or committees and other settings — Conference, Association, national, and other configurations of UCC gatherings — to stimulate thought and conversation about what this thing we call "covenant" means in our life as the church in our time and place. In my wildest dreams, I would love to see this conversation happen in the "building and grounds" committees and choirs of local churches, in Conference staff and board meetings, and among the collegium of our national church but if just a few folks somewhere find it helpful, I will rejoice.

Each session offers a brief "background" piece, which would be most helpful if read in advance of the meeting by participants or at least scanned as the gathering begins.

Then follow some "options for discussion" that the group might want to explore.

In the appendix you will find some of the various definitions or descriptions of covenant I found of interest in my studies, as well as some statements that compare and contrast "covenant" with "contract." Like the entire resource, these are not in any way comprehensive but simply offered for the sake of reflection and conversation. These may be utilized for another discussion session.

Please conclude each conversation with prayer that emerges from your time together. I join you in prayer that the vital notion of covenant will become more meaningful and powerful in your local faith community and in our United Church of Christ as we seek to serve God's mission together. I agree with T. S. Eliot that real life is life *together* and seeking to live in covenant with God and one another can make that life possible and fruitful for us and for God's work in the world.

With thanks to the Illinois Conference
for the sabbatical time spent on this study

Session 1

Covenant in
the Hebrew Testament

According to some scholars, "covenant is the single most overriding theme of the Old Testament." Certainly the frequency of the word's occurrence witnesses to this claim: a computer word search of "covenant" (in the NRSV) yielded 326 instances of just the singular noun "covenant" in the Old Testament.

The Hebrew word most commonly translated covenant, *berith,* may come from an ancient Semitic word meaning "to fetter." In our canon (the Bible as we have received it, after centuries of editing, selecting, translating, and placing it in order by our faith parents), the first occasion of the use of covenant occurs in the story of Noah, in Genesis 6:18. After God has decided to flood the earth because of its corruption and given Noah ark-building directions, God says, "But I will establish my covenant with you; and you shall come into the ark." Noah obeys God and after the flood builds an altar for God. Then God fills out that first slim covenant, going far beyond the rescue of Noah and his family. The covenant God announces (Gen. 9:8–17) is with Noah and his descendants but also "with every living creature...all future generations..." and even "between me and the earth." To these all, God promises an "everlasting covenant" never again to flood the earth. God even places the rainbow as a divine Post-It note to remind God of the promise. This covenant is purely God-initiated and God-committed. Nothing is asked or demanded of Noah or the earth creatures or the earth itself. This is purely God's covenantal promise.

Covenant next takes center stage in the story of God's relationship with Abram and Sarai, beginning with Genesis 15:18: "On that day the Lord made a covenant with Abram...." This covenant is made in the context of a ritual in which animals were killed and divided in two pieces, between which a "flaming torch" passes. I mention this because there is an interesting aspect of ancient covenant making that has to do with making a "space between" (a translation of another covenant root word, *biritim*) — but we'll come back to that in another section.

The God-Abraham covenant is richly developed in Genesis 17. If you read it through you will find no fewer than eleven appearances of the word, a sure sign of the importance covenant carries in the story and in scripture. The covenant with Abraham becomes the foundational covenant that carries throughout the story of Israel, with God's promises of land, descendants, and God's own presence. Here are the basic elements:

> 17:7 *God's part:* "I will establish my covenant between me and you, and your offspring after you throughout their generations, an everlasting covenant, to be God to you and to your offspring after you. And I will give to you, and to your offspring after you, the land where you are now an alien...."

> 17:9 *Abraham's part:* "As for you, you shall keep my covenant, you and your offspring after you

throughout their generations..." [the details of circumcision are developed here, establishing the covenant "in your flesh..."].

Then, in verse 16, God makes another promise that makes possible the fulfillment of all the other promises (to the generations): in spite of the advanced ages of Sarah and Abraham, long past childbearing years, God promises a son, with whom the covenant will move into the future. God keeps the promise in the birth of Isaac, tests the covenant in calling for the son's sacrifice (Genesis 22), and responds to Abraham's faithfulness by saving the promised future through Isaac. Here is set, then, the pattern of mutual faithfulness that God intends in all future relationship with humankind.

And God remembers — God *always* remembers — the promises of the covenant. In Exodus 2:24, hearing the cries of the enslaved Israelites, God "remembered his covenant with Abraham, Isaac, and Jacob" and delivered them. At Sinai, God reminds the people of the covenant (Exod. 19:5) and of God's deliverance (20:1 "I am the Lord your God, who brought you out of the land of Egypt") and then provides the detailed body of commands and consequences of failing to obey that are part of the Sinai covenant.

A note here: scholars have long observed the similarity between the biblical covenants and the form of treaties in the ancient Near East. These treaties were at times between relatively equal entities but often between a conquering king and the subject people or as land grants to favored ones. These sovereign-people covenant formats closely resemble the Old Testament covenant patterns, with the truly Sovereign God reminding the people of what God has done, what God will do, and what is expected of the covenant people.

The Abrahamic and Sinai covenants — and to a lesser extent according to a number of references, the covenant with Noah — become the strong threads upon which Israel's life with God is woven in unfolding eras. The scriptures tell the story of God's constant faithfulness (*hesed,* "steadfast love") to the covenant along with the constant unfaithfulness of the human covenant partners. The kings of Israel are measured by their faithfulness (or lack of same); the prophets remind the people of the covenant and hold them accountable for the consequences of covenant breaking. Over and over again, God reminds and pleads with the people for their part of the covenant: to honor God and to live justly.

The covenant promise given through the prophet Jeremiah to the defeated and exiled people powerfully offers a future hope even for those who have repeatedly broken their covenant with God:

> The days are surely coming, says the Lord, when I will make a new covenant with the house of Israel and the house of Judah. It will not be like the covenant that I made with their ancestors when I took them by the hand to bring them out of the land of Egypt — a covenant that they broke.... But this is the covenant that I will make...: I will put my law within them, and I will write it on their hearts and I will be their God and they will be my people. (Jer. 31:31–33)

Options for Discussion

1. One scholar has said that the biblical covenant "was used to found a people, making their moral commitment to one another far stronger and enduring than that of a vassal to an imperial overlord" (Elazar, 25). Covenant in the Old Testament refers almost always to the covenant between God and the people (almost three hundred of the Old Testament uses are about the God-people covenant). How does the covenant with God create a moral commitment *among* the people?

2. Among those few human-human covenants are two of particular interest. Read the related texts and see what characterizes these two quite different interhuman stories. How are they different or similar? What is God's role in these interpersonal covenants? What role does conflict play in these covenant stories?

   - Genesis 31 (especially vv. 43–54). The covenant between Jacob and Laban.

   - 1 Samuel 18, 1–4; 20:1–17. The covenant between David and Jonathan.

3. Read the Jeremiah 31 covenant promise again. How do you imagine the people in exile heard that promise after they had felt abandoned by God? Can you think of any contemporary situations in which people might question God's faithfulness to the covenant?

Session 2

Covenant in
the New Testament

While the emphasis on God's initiation of covenant certainly continues in the New Testament, some new dimensions of covenant come to us in the "testament" of Jesus.

The very title "testament" for the two parts of Christian scripture witnesses to the importance of the notion of covenant in our scriptural tradition. When the Hebrew Bible was translated into Greek, the translators chose to translate *berith* (the Hebrew word for covenant) with the Greek word *diatheke,* which means literally "will" or "testament," to indicate that covenant is always about God's initiative and will. Then when the Greek Bible was translated into Latin, *diatheke* became *testamentum* and the scriptures became known as the Old and New Testaments — or Old and New Covenants.

In the book of Hebrews, the possible translation of *diatheke* as both "covenant" and "will" (in the sense of "last will and testament") becomes interesting because the NRSV translators decided to translate *diatheke* in Hebrews 9:15 this way: "For this reason he is the mediator of a new *covenant* . . . " but in v. 16 as "Where a *will* is involved, the death of the one who made it must be established." Some scholars interpret these decisions as intending to emphasize that covenant in the New Testament has to do with the singular "will" of God through Jesus and not an agreement between two (equal) parties.

Of the only thirty-one uses of "covenant" or "covenants" in the New Testament, at least seven are quotations from the Hebrew testament. Only four are in the Gospels — two in Luke, one each in Matthew and Mark, and none at all in John. The first Lucan use is in the prophecy of Zechariah (God has "remembered his holy covenant" in 1:72) and makes a wonderful bridge between the Jewish covenant and the later announced "new covenant." The other Gospel uses are, of course, in the remembered words of Jesus at supper with his friends: "this is my blood of the covenant..." (Matt. 26:28, Mark 14:24). Luke writes it differently and adds "new": "This cup that is poured out for you is the new covenant in my blood...."

In the first letter to the church at Corinth, Paul reports that he "received" and now hands on the institution of the Lord's Supper using the Lucan remembered words of Jesus, "the new covenant in my blood." Some believe this "receiving" suggests that even before Paul, the earliest Christians were using "new covenant" language for the new relationship between God and the people given through the life, death, and resurrection of Jesus.

Paul explores the whole relationship between the "old" and the "new" covenant, particularly in Galatians 3–4. It is a somewhat tortuously developed study in which Paul attempts to grapple with the promises of God to Abraham (which Paul seems to see as the primal covenant) and the "law" given on Sinai, which he sees as constricting God's people. In Jesus, Paul sees God renewing and fulfilling the "promises" to Abraham, giving life to God's people. Perhaps the clearest statement of the entire matter comes to us in 2 Corinthians 3:5b–6:

"our competence is from God, who has made us competent to be ministers of a new covenant, not of letter but of spirit; for the letter kills, but the Spirit gives life." Here Paul also places us, the church, in the new covenant picture.

By far the fullest and sometimes most mystifying presentation of covenant in the New Testament is in the book of Hebrews, where there are sixteen references to covenant. The author of Hebrews was writing, many agree, to Jewish Christians struggling with the relationship between their Jewish faith tradition and this new faith. So the author draws on many Hebrew Testament texts, such as Jeremiah 31, to demonstrate God's intent to give a new covenant (Heb. 8:8) and, according to Hebrews, a "better covenant." Jesus, to the author, is the "mediator" of the new covenant, and his death becomes the once-and-for-all sacrifice for what is now an everlasting covenant, putting an end to the cult of sacrifice.

Note: While rich in imagery and use of scripture, the Hebrews case is complex and quite technical, for its specific historical context. Some who claim that the new covenant abrogates or negates God's covenant with the Jews have drawn material in Hebrews out of context and done grievous harm. Such claims have contributed to centuries of deadly anti-Semitism still with us today. There is no time here to go into the counterclaim that the new covenant fulfills but does not abrogate God's covenant with the Jewish people but you can find the UCC General Synod Resolution affirming that claim in the minutes of the 16th General Synod (1987).

Considering our most common contemporary UCC uses of "covenant" as being about our interpersonal and interchurch relationships, it is interesting to observe that none of the New Testament uses are *explicitly* about interhuman relationships per se (like David and Jonathan or Jacob and Laban in the Hebrew testament). However, in Paul's letter to the Ephesians, the Gentiles at Ephesus are first described as "strangers to the covenants of promise" (Eph. 2:12), but then through Christ (and implicitly the new covenant) they become part of the one body, strangers no longer but citizens of the household of God and thus parties to the covenant.

The tight focus of the New Testament uses of "covenant" make one thing very clear: the new covenant is all about Jesus and the gift of life through his life.

Options for Discussion

1. Can you imagine yourselves at the table with Jesus when he blessed the traditional cup of wine and then said to them, "This is my blood of the covenant"? As a Jewish person in that moment, what thoughts or feelings might you have had about his use of "covenant" in that way?

2. Paul says in 2 Corinthians 3:6 that God has "made us competent to be ministers of a new covenant" (read vv. 4–6). What does that mean to you? Do you feel "competent" to be ministers of a new covenant? How might that competency inform your leadership role in the church?

3. Some of us in the mainline church are uncomfortable with the emphasis on "blood" in these New Testament covenant texts. What do you make of the relationship between the metaphor of blood and covenant?

Session 3

God the Covenant Maker

In a 1998 lecture, Rabbi David Hartman offered this thought-provoking statement:

> The covenant is a concrete expression of the principle of divine self-limitation that makes room for the human — the "other" — in the creation of history.

Hartman contends that covenant making distinguishes our God in God's willingness to limit God's own power. When we stop to think about this, it *is* utterly amazing. Really, just think about it! I once saw a teenager wearing a T-shirt that announced "It's All About Me!" But for people of faith, the only one who would have a right to claim that "it's all about me" is God, the maker of all creation, the sovereign one, the giver of life. But that very God has chosen not to be alone but to be in relationship with humanity from the very beginning. In the very first canonical story of God's covenant with Noah, the covenant God initiates and commits to limits God's own freedom: "Never again shall there be a flood to destroy the earth."

This whole issue of the nature of God is no small thing. In fact, covenant making totally transforms some of our classic notions of god-ness. As UCC scholar Walter Brueggemann reminds us (in a 1979 General Synod address), in the ancient world and in many churches today, god-ness is described only by "omni" words like omnipotence, omniscience, etc. Such gods are all about using that omni-power over others, with no need to care for what others want or need. Such gods are remote and heavily into control. But our God? Our covenant-making God posts rainbow notes to remind Godself of those self-imposed limits. Our God offers land and a future to a landless, futureless people. Our God hears the cries of the oppressed and comes to free slaves who proceed to murmur and complain and look for shinier omni-gods to follow. Our God keeps trying, endlessly, to stay in covenant with self-centered kings and with consistently covenant-breaking people. And our God comes to us and shares our common lot in Jesus, who "emptied himself... and being found in human form, he humbled himself and became obedient to the point of death — even death on a cross" (Phil. 2:6–8). In that emptying, humbling, obedience, death, and resurrection, God in Jesus gives us a new covenant for new life. In that new life, we know that our God is indeed "with us," Immanuel.

Our God, the God Christians know best through Jesus the Christ, turns all ideas about God upside down. Here's how Brueggemann said it:

> What emerges [from this covenant-making God's behavior] is a theological revolution. This God is not marked by power but by faithfulness and vulnerability. This God resolves to be with and stay with and depend upon the resources, judgments, and capacities of God's new covenant partner. Covenant means to locate the power for life, not in self, but in the commitment, giving, and caring of the other ones....

The God who makes covenant with us is best charac-
terized by faithfulness. Another biblical way of speaking
of that faithfulness is "steadfast love." Psalms 25 (v. 1),
89 (v. 28), and 106 (v. 45) testify to this consistent covenant keeping, even in the face of rejection by God's
covenant partners. Psalm 106, for instance, remembers
how God delivered the unfaithful wilderness wanderers:

> Many times God delivered them, but they were
>   rebellious in their purposes. . . .
> Nevertheless God regarded their distress when
>   God heard their cry.
> For their sake God remembered God's covenant,
>   and showed compassion according to the
>   abundance of God's steadfast love.
>
> (vv. 43–46)

Our God "hangs in" with God's beloved ones endlessly. But our covenant-making God is not without
expectations of us as covenant partners. This same God
who bends, negotiates, and keeps on keeping on has an
equal commitment to mutual accountability to which
the scriptures also testify. There are pages and pages
of covenantal expectations in the Sinai covenant, but
perhaps the simplest and most compelling statement
puts it best: "I will be their God and they will be my
people" (Jer. 31:33). To promise to remain our God,
our persistent and faithful covenant partner, is the high-
est commitment for one who could, in god-ness, turn
away. But to be God's people carries all kinds of weight
and expectation as well. Our part is to have no other
gods — not wealth, not comfort, not military might,
nothing is to come between us and our true God. And
we are to live our lives in ways that show we are indeed
God's people, covenant partners with the God of love
and justice and peace.

Along with the expectation of accountability comes one further characteristic of our covenant God that is not nearly as warming to our hearts as God's eternal faithfulness, though without that faithfulness we could not even contemplate this trait. Our covenant-making God allows the unfolding of consequences from human covenant breaking. The "blessings" of keeping covenant in the Sinai story are accompanied by "curses" or consequences (see Deuteronomy 7–9, for instance) of breaking covenant. King Solomon — and remember that the kings of Israel represent the whole people — learned just how serious God is about this (1 Kings 11:9–11):

> Then the Lord was angry with Solomon, because his heart had turned away from the Lord, the God of Israel, who had appeared to him twice, and had commanded him concerning this matter, that he should not follow other gods; but he did not observe what the Lord commanded. Therefore the Lord said to Solomon, "Since this has been your mind and you have not kept my covenant and my statutes . . . I will surely tear the kingdom from you and give it to your servant."

So our covenant-making God is all about relationship, faithfulness and self-yielding. But that same God holds us accountable and, perhaps weeping like Rachel, permits the consequences of human unfaithfulness to unfold — but always with a promise of never abandoning us. This is truly an amazing God.

Options for Discussion

1. Both of the scholars named here, Hartman and
   Brueggemann, dangle another surprising characteristic of God in front of us: the notion that
   our covenant-making God might "depend upon"
   or even "need" this relationship with humanity.
   Hartman suggests that in making covenants with
   humanity, God "needs the cooperation of human
   beings to achieve the divine vision for history."
   What do you think of that idea? What might that
   notion mean for your understanding of God? Of
   yourself? Of your church?

2. What difference does it make to your life and
   your church setting if God is a covenant-making
   God who is self-giving and faithful but who also
   holds us accountable and permits us to experience
   consequences of our covenant breaking?

Covenant in
Our UCC Heritage

Note: If your group hasn't already done a quick review of United Church of Christ history and polity (how we govern ourselves), it would be good to do so prior to this session as I'm going to assume a basic knowledge.

As we have seen, the scriptural covenantal tradition is "all about God." Out of hundreds of biblical references to covenant, only a few are clearly primarily about human relationships. Covenant is "God's thing" — God initiates the covenantal relationship with humanity, God goes to great lengths to stay in covenantal relationship, even to sharing our common human life in Jesus, creating a new covenant.

So when, how, and why did the predominant referent of the word "covenant" become our current one — about covenants among people and, in the United Church of Christ, among the settings of our church? It would take a treatise to answer those questions in depth. One source cites as a church covenant precursor early first- and second-century church references to an oath that new (and probably Gentile) Christians took, agreeing to abide by certain practices. But in terms of covenant among people in the life of the church, it seems that the real transition came with the Reformation. Surely the leaders of the Reformation movement kept foremost reference to the divine covenant. It was, however, in their writing and thinking about God's covenant of grace that questions began to emerge that related to the nature of the church and who truly was a party to the covenant (or the "elect," with key rights in leadership, etc.), which always also means asking who is not "in" the covenant (and not "the elect").

Emerging from that Reformation era, our four primary denominational parent bodies (remembering that the UCC now also includes several other key influential and discrete bodies) began to use covenant language to consider not only their life with God but what their covenant life with God meant to their life with one another as the church. Randi Walker tells us that "the Congregational, Reformed, Christian, and Evangelical traditions all had within their understandings of the nature and purpose of the church some idea of a covenantal relationship both of the church with God and the church and its people with one another" (133). Much of that covenantal background can be traced to European Reformers, particularly John Calvin, who emphasized that God's covenant is a covenant of grace (as humanity repeatedly fails to keep our part of the covenant) and that the divine covenant is sealed in the sacraments of the church: baptism and Eucharist (or communion).

A key figure in the move from our covenant with God to the covenant with one another is Robert Browne, a Puritan leader, who in the late sixteenth century articulated the covenant of an individual Christian with God as connected to relationships among Christians as church. From Browne we hear an emphasis that needs, in my view, to be claimed anew by us: the covenant with God is the primal covenant from which our human covenants are derived and by which they are shaped. The language is mine but partly drawn from discussions of Browne's writing. In covenant making, Christians give themselves first to God and then to one another (paraphrase of 2 Cor. 8:5). A way of thinking about this relationship is that if we are each in a relationship of covenantal grace with God, then God stands at the center of us all and we, like spokes on a wheel, find ourselves inextricably linked to one another in relationships that need endless development in further covenant making.

From that kind of understanding about our covenant with God has emerged a deep understanding of the church as a covenant people. In fact, Richard Mather, in a bit of English controversy about church and covenant, wrote in 1643, "By entering into Covenant with God, a people come to be the Lord's people, that is to say, his Church..." (Barton, 64). It is, in this view, the covenant relationship with God that creates the church and, in turn, creates a covenantal relationship among the people who are the church. The Salem Church Covenant of 1629 was early among many other church covenants. The simplicity of this covenant gives it power that still stands as a model for church life:

> We covenant with the Lord and one with another; and doe bynd ourselves in the presence of God, to walke together in all his waies, according as he is pleased to reveale himself unto us in his Blessed word of truth. (as it appears in Barton, 60)

Over the years, the churches that became Congregational developed local church covenants that became more and more complex, with all kinds of detail about behavior and practices of membership. Theological discussion continued about who is among the "elect" in the church. These developments spilled into and interacted mutually with the emergence of democratic political governance in the colonies. The original Puritan ideal of a theocracy (for the Puritans literally saw themselves as the new Israel in renewed covenant with God in the Promised Land) conflicted (because of claims of rule only by those "elected") with emerging notions of governance by all the people. Gradually these covenant concepts emerged in the increasingly distinct but historically related ideas of secular democratic governance and covenanted life of autonomous congregations.

But covenant was not just about life *within* congregations. The idea of covenant in the United States early began to include life *among* congregations, as well. Some among us today want to claim that the Congregational strand of our heritage was purely local, emphasizing local autonomy, an idea we'll explore more in the next section. But Walker reminds us that as early as 1648, the Cambridge Platform formed Congregational synods and councils of churches for mutual support and even for "debating and determining 'controversies of faith and cases of conscience'" (Walker, 140). In 1728, German Reformed churches in Pennsylvania sought a covenantal relationship with Dutch Reformed churches to maintain their sense of identity. In 1840, the Evangelical churches in Missouri and surrounding region met for mutual "acquaintance" and to make a "covenant of fraternal fellowship." Of all the strands of our heritage, the Christian tradition apparently made the least of covenant as creating relationships among congregations (perhaps in concern for yielding of congregational independence) but because of a commitment to the unity of the church, through God's divine covenant, Christian churches as well formed relationships in a "General Convention."

This rich covenantal heritage has shaped who we are now as the United Church of Christ, as will be explored further in following sections.

Options for Discussion

1. Does your local church have history rooted in one of the four main streams that became the United Church of Christ in 1957? How has covenant become or not become part of your congregation's life out of that history? If yours is a post-1957-born congregation, has covenant been part of your church's life? If so, how?

2. The word "covenant" entered United Church of Christ life in a formal way with the adoption of the 1959 Statement of Faith, which now in the form of a doxology reads: "You bestow upon us your holy Spirit, creating and renewing the church of Jesus Christ, binding in covenant faithful people of all ages, tongues and races...." How does that statement speak to you or for you now? Does it effectively express the historic role of covenant in our UCC heritage? Disregarding for now discussions of the statement's length, what, if anything, would you add to the Statement of Faith if you wanted to expand what it says about covenant?

Session 5

Our Covenant as the Wider United Church of Christ

The ministry in which I serve as a Conference minister sets my colleagues and me at a lively intersection of church life, between the local church and the national setting (plus Associations, where those exist). It is a ministry that calls for keeping communication flowing in all directions, nurturing relationships, articulating and supporting the covenantal relationships, etc. So I admit here and now that I have an investment in this part of our conversation. But please remember that I have lived and served in just about every setting of this United Church of Christ. (Note that in our Constitution, "setting" and "expression" are intentionally used to distinguish from "levels," which suggest hierarchy.) I love *all* expressions of our church, blessings and curses combined — and all of our settings carry both. So see what you think of my "case" for the covenants among our settings and then feel free to argue, write another case, whatever — that's so UCC!

Actually, the "case" is not mine; it is made very well in the current Constitution and Bylaws of the United Church of Christ. And a longer, excellent narration of the background and contemporary use of covenant in the UCC is made by Randi Walker in chapter 5 of her very helpful book, *The Evolution of a UCC Style*. But for the sake of this discussion, let me draw on Walker and the Constitution as well as other sources to present some basics for your consideration.

As Walker says, "For many, the key concept in our ecclesiology is contained in the Constitution and Bylaws of the United Church of Christ, and some might argue that this statement is the closest thing we have in the UCC to a dogma ... "! Here is a portion of that statement:

> (Article V, paragraph 18) The autonomy of the Local Church is inherent and modifiable only by its own action. Nothing in this Constitution and the Bylaws of the United Church of Christ shall destroy or limit the right of each Local Church to continue to operate in the way customary to it; nor shall be construed as giving to the General Synod, or to any Conference or Association now, or at any future time, the power to abridge or impair the autonomy of any Local Church in the management of its own affairs....

That's pretty clear. This statement emerged from the formative conversations of the merger that led to the birth of the United Church of Christ and, I would pose, without it there would be no United Church of Christ, for congregations from our parent families would not have agreed to the union. It is a dearly held value, emerging from the Reformation resistance to both hierarchical church and state entities.

But "congregational autonomy" is not all there is to who we are as the UCC. Paragraph 17 of Article V of the Constitution, titled "Local Churches," *precedes* the one above and says this: "The Local Churches of the United Church of Christ have, in fellowship, a God-given responsibility for that Church, its labors and its extension, even as the United Church of Christ has, in fellowship, a God-given responsibility for the well-being and needs and aspirations of its Local Churches. In mutual Christian concern and in dedication to Jesus Christ, the Head of the Church, the one and the many share in common Christian experience and responsibility."

It has all the makings of a covenant, doesn't it? Clarity of identity of the parties, statements of mutual responsibility — everything but the blessings and curses, even though we live those out. But the word "covenant" did not appear in our Constitution until the 2000 revision. Until then, "covenant" was appealed to regularly by local pastors, lay leaders, and leadership in all wider settings of our church in conversations about how we work together, particularly through challenging times when the temptation to go our separate ways flares up among us. As the restructure of the national setting created five national "Covenanted Ministries" with further relationships through the (then) thirty-nine Conferences, this paragraph was added, giving name and modest definition to the "glue," some have called it, which holds us together (Article III, Covenantal Relationships, paragraph 6):

> Within the United Church of Christ, the various expressions of the church relate to each other in a covenantal manner. Each expression of the church has responsibilities and rights in relation to the others, to the end that the whole church will seek God's will and be faithful to God's mission. Decisions are made in consultation and collaboration among the various parts of the structure. As members of the Body of Christ, each expression of the church is called to honor and respect the work and ministry of each other part. Each expression of the church listens, hears, and carefully considers the

advice, counsel, and requests of others. In this covenant, the various expressions of the United Church of Christ seek to walk together in all God's ways.

Some interesting decisions were made in the wording of this section — the mutual honor and respect, the listening, hearing, and considering are all in the present tense, as if an ongoing and unquestioned reality. While there is room to question that reality, there is value in naming the covenantal reality in which we intend to live, even when, like our biblical faith parents, we regularly break the covenant.

When I teach about this dynamic in our church, I tend to hold out my hands as if they were scales and suggest that we live constantly in the struggle to balance the value of autonomy with the value of mutual covenantal respect and responsibility. And that is true among all the setting and expressions of our church because each is either entirely or substantively "autonomous." So the balancing effort takes place among local churches; between local churches and Associations and Conferences; between Conferences and the national setting; between the ministries of the national setting; and every other way the lines can be drawn. It is a daunting balancing act but, for all our frets and frustrations, for fifty years our United Church of Christ has been a fruitful instrument for God's mission in the midst of the challenging adventure.

An aspect of this whole picture that complicates but also makes possible our continuing covenantal life together is this often forgotten reality: there is no "them" in our wider church. Every expression of the wider United Church of Christ beyond the local church is governed by none other than local church folks. Conferences are made up of nothing more and nothing less than the local churches and authorized ministers within those Conferences — there is no one else, no "them." The national setting of our church is governed by representatives from those very Conferences — lay folk and clergy from local churches making decisions for the wider expressions of the church through the General Synod and the Covenanted Ministry boards. So we are our own covenant partners.

Rev. Oliver Powell once described the United Church of Christ as a "heady, exhilarating, exasperating mix." It is all of that and it is not an easy church in which to serve Christ and God's mission, but I am convinced that our covenantal life together is part of how God wants to teach the world to live. We are a laboratory, a show window for part of God's vision.

Options for Discussion

1. Is "local church autonomy" truly a "dogma" (an authoritative teaching) in the United Church? What are the strengths and what are the hazards of this strongly held value from the perspective of covenant in the setting of the church where you are having this discussion?

2. How do you see the balancing act of covenantal life in the UCC being lived out in your setting of the church?

Session 6

But What about Autonomy and Covenant?

"Autonomy" is a "hot button" word in our church. It is often taken to mean full independence, as if a local church (or any other expression of the church) could stand alone. And of course, every United Church of Christ congregation can find in its surrounding community truly independent "stand-alone" congregations. Some UCC congregations have withdrawn from the denomination out of disagreement with decisions or actions of some other setting to do precisely that. It is inherent in our identity that such an action is possible — in fact it is guaranteed in paragraph 18 of the Constitution of the United Church of Christ.

What, then, is the difference between "autonomy" in the United Church of Christ and such independence? You will not be surprised at my contention that covenant makes the difference. Autonomy in the life of the United Church of Christ draws us into consideration of ideas like freedom and authority in the midst of covenant.

Covenant is all about freedom — but freedom, in fact, to be in relationship. Covenant is first of all about God's freedom. As Walker reminds us, regarding the work of the Reformer John Calvin on covenant, "From our perspective it is sometimes difficult to remember that Calvin's great objective theologically was to defend the freedom of God, not the freedom of the congregation." This is a crucial point, if we discipline ourselves to remember that all of our churchly covenants begin with God's covenant with us. And in that covenant making, we recall, God chose in freedom to limit God's own self to make promises to humanity. (If such a choice is "good enough" for God, why is it so difficult for us?) At the same time, God expected our accountability — while nevertheless leaving us fully free to reject that accountability.

Granted, it is a rather mystifying and somewhat circular discussion. In freedom God chooses to limit God's freedom and freely allows humanity to choose limiting ourselves (to one God, for instance) while being free not to do so. Historically, some have tried to create a wall between God's covenant of grace, unconditional relationship, and "the law," with conditional covenant obligations, in order to give some rigidity to this very fluid life God offers. But as Brueggemann affirms, the neat and conventional antithesis between law and grace is a distortion of faith, because "there are no unconditional or conditional relationships in the gospel, but only relationships of fidelity that prize both freedom and accountability, the two always intertwined and to be negotiated" (*The Covenanted Self*, 44).

That statement articulates well who we are as the United Church of Christ, *a covenantal network of autonomous bodies who "prize both freedom and accountability, the two always intertwined and to be negotiated."* Throughout our history, and particularly since the making of the 1957 union, "negotiating" those realities in our real life together has been the adventure, fraught with challenge, joy, and risk. Each time a congregation calls a pastor, each time the General Synod makes a statement, each time a Conference sets a budget, and in many more moments, we of the United Church of Christ swim in that fluid adventure of autonomous-covenantal life with God and one another.

Such a life requires several things to stay afloat. First, as Brueggemann notes, "covenanting requires maturity to be 'knit together in love'" (*The Covenanted Self,* 11). Such maturity requires developing the art and skill called for in Ephesians 4:15: "But speaking the truth in love, we must grow up in every way into him who is the head, into Christ...." As this is written, our United Church of Christ is preparing to celebrate our fiftieth "birthday" and we are still living into that kind of maturity. Speaking the truth in covenantal love is a great deal more than bland churchy "niceness." It is a rigorous discipline — as is hearing the truth, as another experiences or perceives it, in love. We are swimming in deep water, friends.

A second reality required in living out autonomy within covenant is freely making and then freely living with the choice of being in covenant. That choice means yielding some of one's own power to the "other," the covenant partners. Autonomy in the United Church of Christ is the freedom to yield something of ourselves (or of our setting), our power to do what we please, to the covenantal partner relationship. Elazar expresses this mutual yielding in the God-human relationship in a way that invites our grasp of the need for such yielding in our human covenantal relationships:

> In covenanting with humans, God in effect limits Himself and withdraws somewhat from interfering with them to give them space to be independently human. He grants humans a degree of freedom under the terms of the covenant retaining only the authority to reward or punish the consequences of that freedom at some future date. By the same

token, the humans who bind themselves through
the covenant limit their powers as well. (68)

In our intramural skirmishes in the United Church of
Christ around social or political issues, around governance, etc., it may be helpful for all concerned to
remember that the choice of being in covenant is a
choice to be autonomous in a very different way from
the world's conception of being autonomous or independent. Brueggemann affirms: "I understand covenant
in our own time and place to be a radical alternative
to consumer autonomy, which is the governing ideology
of our society and which invades the life of the church
in debilitating ways." In "consumer autonomy," everything is all about me and mine. The church, our church,
calls us to be attentive to the other and to serve God's
mission through the covenant. Deep water, indeed.

To conclude this section, it may be helpful to consider one case in which a local church yields some of its
authority to another setting of the church. Many local
churches include in their constitutions the provision that
their pastor must be a person with "ministerial standing" (authorization) in the United Church of Christ.
Once that decision is made, the local church has trans-
ferred some authority and yielded some of its power to
the Association of which it is a part, for the authorization of ministers is a function of Associations (or in a few
cases, a Conference acting as an Association). However
the local church has a role to play in the Association,
so it becomes a covenantal partner with itself to the
extent that it participates in the processes of that Association that does the work of authorization. All of which
works very well until a local church disagrees with some
decision of the Association — such as an action to re-
move a minister's standing due to fitness questions. At

that moment, the entire covenantal relationship is tested and a congregation must decide whether it will continue to yield its authority to the covenantal relationship or, perhaps, change its constitution and retain the pastor.

Engaging this autonomous life within covenant can be a rich but also stressful adventure at times among the various expressions of the United Church of Christ. But in our efforts for covenantal faithfulness, we have an opportunity to show the world a "better way" of differing than disengagement and separation. Such covenantal living among autonomous entities can make a powerful witness — or fail to do so — in a world of walled borders and violent power struggles.

Options for Discussion

1. When has the balance of autonomy-covenant become challenging in the experience of your UCC setting? How has it been resolved — or has it? Share one or more examples.

2. Does the constitution of your setting deal with matters of autonomy and covenant? How? Are you satisfied with the way it does so?

Particular Covenants among Us

In addition to the explicit covenant that literally creates the United Church of Christ (expressed in our Constitution), there are some others that exist or may helpfully be created in our life together. In this section, we'll just touch upon several.

We have already mentioned one form of such covenants, the local church or congregational covenant. Following the precedents of covenants like the 1629 Salem Covenant, local churches, particularly and perhaps only in the Congregational tradition, began to write their own covenants of membership or congregational covenants. These ranged from the brief Salem type, often resembling an affirmation of faith, to lengthy and detailed covenants outlining how members may be removed from membership and other intricacies of local church life. (Barton's chapter 10 contains numerous samples of these congregational covenants.) Some United Church of Christ congregations continue to hold such covenants as part of their formative documents. I would suggest that development of new covenantal agreements in any setting of the church could be a rich process.

Such covenants, for instance, might help to clarify expectations of membership in a particular congregation, church council, committee, or wider church governing body, and new members might be invited to "sign on." Developing such a covenant will challenge many of our churches to think in new ways, as we have become unaccustomed to having any clear expectations of members or leaders. A local church might ask, What *do* we really expect of one another as members of this church? A Conference or Association might ask, what do we as churches together expect of the local churches that are part of this Association or Conference? Those are radical questions but just wrestling with them could be lively and thought-provoking in our life together. The relatively new (and I find largely unknown) United Church of Christ *Manual on Church* begins to explore that latter question and is still being developed. You can check it out at *www.ucc.org/ministers/church*.

Another type of covenant that I particularly want to commend is a "behavioral covenant." Early in my wider church ministry, I went to a church in deep conflict with its pastor, and in my naiveté I asked the council leadership, "What can you think of in the Bible that might be helpful as you lead the congregation in this time?" Having served in a fairly biblically literate congregation, I was stunned to be greeted with a resounding silence. Not even something so basic as the word "love" was spoken, much less "covenant." Later I came across a 1992 Presbyterian resource page titled "Seeking to Be Faithful Together: Guidelines for Presbyterians during Times of Disagreement." The piece invited participants to promise to follow ten biblically based guidelines, for example, "to resist name-calling or labeling of others," based on the Ephesians "speaking the truth in love" text. Such guidelines can be helpful in a situation of church conflict, which we sometimes forget is normal and consistent with our early church heritage; after all, the New

Testament was written, as Parker Palmer has said, "in the caldron of conflict."

My ministry offered many opportunities to be in ministry with folks in such situations so I began to adapt the guidelines and offer them to local leaders, urging them to begin those painful congregational meetings about a conflict issue with reflection on such guidelines and agreement that the group present will seek to live by them. In other words, to make a covenant. Where tried, it has been helpful just to begin the gathering with something other than the "presenting problem" and to remind the congregation who they are in faith.

Gilbert Rendle's excellent Alban Institute book *Behavioral Covenants in Congregations* has provided a helpful title to this kind of covenant. In the Illinois Conference, when we prepared to vote on a resolution that the Conference declare itself an Open and Affirming Conference, the Conference Council adapted versions of what we now call a behavioral covenant and offered the result to the Conference delegates for their approval. I am convinced that the covenant, along with other efforts, helped provide a context in which the conflicts among us could be dealt with (not hidden or eliminated) in faithful ways that reflected our covenantal identity with God and with one another. We now adopt a Covenant of Behavior at each Conference annual meeting.

When I introduce the idea of a behavioral covenant to the leadership of a church in conflict or wrestling with some difficult issue such as disagreement about some social issue, I emphasize that the covenant is not a "magic incantation" and has value only if the leadership and the participants are committed to it. (Ideally, a congregation would develop and adopt such a covenant before a particular conflict emerges but that isn't common, I fear.) Further, the leadership must be prepared to remind those present of the covenant when someone strays far from its guidance, calling the group into account for the covenant. Yes, this is an alien practice in most of our churches, but it is a spiritual discipline that can enrich our life together.

In his book, Rendle offers other helpful models of congregational covenants that could be utilized in any setting of the United Church of Christ, such as a behavioral covenant for staff that includes agreements like "We promise to express criticism and negative feelings first to the person, not to others." There may be many situations in which such particular covenants are useful if we would bump up the notion of covenant in our minds.

Options for Discussion

1. Does your local church (or other church setting) currently have any explicit covenantal expressions? If so, is it ever lifted up in your common life? Is it in a form that is still relevant to your life together? If not, how would you adapt it?

2. If you have no explicit covenantal expressions, do you think such a covenant might be helpful? What kind?

Session 8

Covenant Making and Covenant Renewal

The practice of explicit covenant making seems to have faded recently in our United Church of Christ life together. As hinted in session 7, I suspect that one reason is our UCC, or perhaps human, resistance to making anything in our relationships that firm or expectations so clear. Perhaps a way of reclaiming this tradition and reframing covenant in new ways as central to our church life is to recall the scriptural heritage of covenant making and covenant renewal as acts of worship.

From that first covenant with Noah, covenant making has involved human acts of worship. Following the end of the flooding in Genesis 8, Noah "built an altar to the Lord." The story tells us that God is so pleased with this act of worship that the covenant promised in 6:18 is given substance, from God's side, in 8:21–22 and chapter 9. The covenant with Abraham in Genesis 17 is concluded with the "sign of the covenant" in circumcision, to this day an act of worship in the Jewish community. The covenant between Laban and Jacob, bringing an end to their conflict, is marked by the ritual building of a pillar and a "heap" of stones, by prayer, by the making of a sacrifice, and by sharing bread in the community. The Sinai covenant in Genesis 19 is formalized in a communal response: "Everything that the

Lord has spoken we will do," and the people are consecrated by God's presence. And, of course, most of the New Testament covenant references occur in relationship to the Lord's supper: "This cup is the new covenant in my blood..." (1 Cor. 11:25).

Worship is central in covenant making in scripture but also in covenant renewal. After the Israelites had strayed from the covenant as witnessed in their worship of the golden calf, a service of repentance is followed (in Genesis 34) by a new covenant-making service. And again, when the tribes of Israel are "east of Jordan," Joshua gathers them at Shechem, tells them the story of God's faithfulness and gifts, and calls them to decide if they will serve the Lord in faithful covenant (Josh. 24:1–28). Here again, there is a ritualized quality to the words, with Joshua and the people sharing in what sounds like a responsive reading.

For a model from another part of our history, we might look again at the Salem Covenant:

> We covenant with the Lord and one with another; and doe bynd ourselves in the presence of God, to walke together in all his waies, according as he is pleased to reveale himself unto us in his Blessed word of truth. (as it appears in Barton, 60)

The brevity and clarity suggest the ease of using this rich covenant in worship, and though I have no way of knowing if that was done, I would be surprised if it was not. Some years ago, a UCC anniversary video included a sung version of this covenant, "We Will Walk Together..."

What if the settings of the United Church of Christ renewed our covenant relationships with God and one another in more explicit ways than is common among us — naming the reality of our covenantal roles, clarifying the content of the covenant and creating ways of reminding one another of those covenants — with symbols (a heap of stones?) or by citing or even re-citing elements of the covenant in worship or to open ministry team gatherings? What if congregations developed membership covenants as discussed in session 7 and then annually invited all to join in covenant renewal, perhaps at Pentecost? We come very close to covenant renewal when a congregation welcomes confirmands or new members, but we rarely name what we are doing as covenant nor do we set it in the framework of God's covenant faithfulness with us.

The same opportunity exists for wider church settings — the very process of identifying elements that need covenant clarification might itself be valuable. What are the blessings of the covenant relationships among us? What are the expectations? What are the consequences when covenant is broken (or are there any)? What an adventure addressing those questions can be in our UCC life together!

There are many possibilities. But I need to confess that I fear our United Church of Christ commitment to freedom has lately become a commitment to avoiding covenantal clarity. If (and yes, this is a large "if") we accept that covenant is very much about freedom, including the freedom to yield some of that freedom to make possible a life-giving, mission-strengthening relationship, then we need to learn afresh how to name the specifics of some of our covenants and formalize them and renew them in meaningful worship moments. Certainly such experiences risk the greatly feared slippery slopes to the kind of legalism our faith parents resisted with their lives and livelihoods. But at this time in our

United Church of Christ history and in our culture of individualism and idolatry of "me and mine," I contend that it may be time for us to step up to the covenantal plate and make new expressions of what we mean by our covenantal relationships in and among our various settings. Such new covenants, expressed with clarity and lived in faithfulness, could become part of the witness we make to the world. Moreover, they enter our hearts more deeply when we speak the words often, engage in actions like signing membership covenants, or tell our covenant story. With our focus on our covenant-making God and God's incredible faithfulness and flexibility — repeatedly revising and renewing relationship with us even when we have broken covenant — I believe we can safely continue the adventure with better positioned clarity but without sliding down the feared slope.

Options for Discussion

1. Does your setting of the church have any documented covenant expressions, like a congregational covenant? Is it used in worship? Where can it be found? Are new members introduced to it? Do you think most members would still affirm it? What parts might be claimed the most fully and what might need to be changed?

2. If your setting of the church does not to your knowledge have a clear covenantal statement, what elements would you want to see named in such a covenant?

3. Two yoked rural churches have a banner hanging in the sanctuaries showing a road between the two buildings to symbolize their covenantal

relationship. What symbols might be created to visibly express the covenants in your setting or covenants of your setting with other UCC bodies? What might it be like if folks entering the space of your UCC church setting had to walk around a "heap of stones" for the next few gatherings?

So What Is Covenant to Us?

Certainly by now, if your group has spent time reflecting on covenant during these sessions, I could well leave this section with just the title and invite you to respond to the question it asks with no further word from me. But I can't resist sharing some further — and final — thoughts that might "salt" your conversation. They will be just "chunks" of thought and questions to stir your own thoughts and discussion.

• As we have said, the "first" covenant named in our canon of scriptures is God's generous, one-sided covenant with all of humanity and creation through the covenant with Noah. And as we have also said, the reality of all creation and humanity being in that covenantal relationship with God, whether acknowledged or not, brings all of those elements into relationship as well — all of humanity, humanity with creation, etc. Whether we or they like it or not! What are the implications for you, for your setting of the church, for our United Church of Christ, that God has entered into covenant with *all* of creation, yielding some of God's own freedom and power to do so? What does that suggest about our power relationships? About our relationship to all creation? To global humanity? A caution here: some simple UCC easy answer about "well, we need to do justice..."

is not enough. Get specific. What could this ancient and ongoing covenantal action by God mean in our church practices? In our homes? In our life as a denomination? Does it threaten anything in our status quo? Or does it mean anything at all to us?

• Covenant making can do constructive work by clarifying the unique identities and differences among us as well as clarifying how we are related to one another. Remember that forms of the Hebrew word often translated "covenant" (*brit*) can mean to cut or to make a space between (as Abraham did with the sacrificed animals in Genesis 15). Covenant in our time can be a way to carve out our own identities (or that of our UCC setting) as well as creating a bond (as Abraham then did in binding the halves together in the ritual). As Elazar says, a covenant "both divides and binds . . . clarifies and institutionalizes both the distinctions between or separate identities of the partners and their linkage" (65). How could that kind of dual benefit of a covenant be useful in your setting's relationship with other settings of the United Church of Christ?

• Seeing covenant from that perspective, as not only "binding" but also clarifying separateness and identity, can be useful in creating what Elazar calls a "framework for dialogue." The covenant-making process can open opportunities for all involved in some kind of conflict or disagreement to name how they see themselves and how they see the relationship, the linkage. In a current interfaith conversation in which I am involved, among Muslims, Christians, and Jews (all people of the covenant in heritage), we who are participating find ourselves identifying who we are (and who we are not) more clearly as we try also to listen to and hear the self-identification of the other. That part of the conversation is essential before we can also say how we might work together for peace because it sets some appropriate limits right from the beginning. In this case, for instance, we might discover that while we share a common connection to Abraham, we each trace a different line of meaning from that connection, which might inform our differences as much as our similarities.

- Each occasion of constitutional change or that often dreaded word "restructure" can open up possibilities of covenant making and transform what could be mere bureaucratic activity into powerful experiences of faith. Seeing each suggestion of such changes as an *opportunity* to explore covenant in our life together can tilt the way we enter or live into such change experiences. Is your UCC setting in the midst of such change? How might notions of covenant inform or transform that process?

- Covenant offers the gift of flexibility within structure rather than rigidity. If, indeed, part of our UCC resistance to contemporary covenant making with clear content of expectations is rooted in our fear of getting "locked in" to some kind of legalism, we have only to look at God's regular willingness to renew, restate, and even revise the covenant — as in Jeremiah 31 and the "new covenant" in Jesus. It has been some time since our church covenantal life has been written in literal stone, and we could be enriched by recognizing that our covenants can be lived in with commitment while knowing that they can also be revised and renewed, following God's model.

- Whenever Christians meet at the table of Jesus, we are entering a covenantal moment. How can our celebrations of the Eucharist or communion be more clearly or meaningfully covenantal in expression and experience? What *really* is happening among all the participants when we share from the common loaf and from the cup of the new covenant?

Finally, with the help of Walter Brueggemann ("The Risk of Heaven, the Possibility of Earth," address to the Twelfth General Synod), I ask you now if covenant can helpfully be the "governing metaphor of our life"? God has "risked" God's freedom and power in the covenants of the Old Testament and God has risked God's own self in Jesus Christ. God's risks and willingness to yield power and freedom for the sake of relationship invite us to risk and yield and to ask if we believe this:

> Covenanting is possible on the earth. It is possible to practice life in a new way, in family and in church, in seminaries and in boards and agencies. It is possible to practice employment and housing, sexuality and education, medicine and energy in covenantal ways, even on this earth. That is no small task and no mean vision. And in adopting this theme, we declare to each other that we believe a radical reorientation of power relations among us is possible and is promised in the gospel. (GS12 minutes, 124)

If we believe this, as people of a covenant-making God, perhaps, just perhaps, we can become agents of transformation toward God's vision of covenant, when all the people of the earth will live in harmony. Living actively and to the best of our human ability in the adventure of covenant can be our gift, as the United Church of Christ, to our God and to God's world. Thank you for sharing part of the adventure with me.

Appendix

Brief Definitions and Descriptions of Covenant

A suggestion for use as an extra session on covenant: Read the following and ask members of the group to identify one or two statements or even words or phrases that bring a new insight or raise a new thought or question about covenant. Then discuss.

Interpreter's Bible Dictionary, 188:

* "Covenant. An agreement between two or more persons.... The Hebrew word for covenant is *berith,* which has the etymological meaning of 'a bond.'"

Walter Brueggemann, *The Covenanted Self,* 1:

* "I understand covenant in our own time and place to be a radical alternative to consumer autonomy, which is the governing ideology of our society and which invades the life of the church in debilitating ways."

Walter Brueggemann, "The Risk of Heaven, the Possibility of Earth," Twelfth General Synod Minutes, 1979, 124:

* "The word means many things. But as a beginning it means this much:a way of being committed to each

other as God is committed to us, a way of being defined by, accountable to and responsible for each other. God has made that deep and abiding commitment to us. And we affirm that our pilgrimage together is marked by such a costly, disciplined and abiding commitment."

David Hartman, "The Theological Significance of Israel:

♦ "Covenant is a concrete expression of the principle of divine self-limitation that makes room for the human — the 'other' — in the creation of history."

Samuel E. Balentine, *The Torah's Vision of Worship,* 123:

♦ "God's inauguration of covenant — just like God's creation of the world — finds its ultimate goal in Israel's empowerment to join God in a relationship of creaturely partnership."

Daniel Elazar, *Covenant and Polity in Biblical Israel:*

♦ "Politically a covenant involves a coming together (con-gregation) of basically equal humans who consent with one another through a morally binding pact supported by a transcendent power, establishing with the partners a new framework or setting them on the road to a new task that can only be dissolved by mutual agreement of all the parties to it." (1)

♦ "A covenant is a morally informed agreement or pact based upon voluntary consent, established by mutual oaths or promises, involving or witnessed by some transcendent higher authority, between peoples or parties having independent status, equal in connection with the purposes of the pact, that provides for joint action or obligation to achieve defined ends (limited or comprehensive) under conditions of mutual respect, which protect the individual integrities of all the parties to it." (23)

- "In its theological form, covenant embodies the idea that relationships between God and humanity are based upon morally sustained compacts of mutual promise and obligation." (23)

- "In all its forms, the key focus of covenant is on *relationships*. A covenant is the constitutionalization of a relationship." (24)

- "In covenanting with humans, God in effect limits Himself and withdraws somewhat from interfering with them to give them space to be independently human. He grants humans a degree of freedom under the terms of the covenant retaining only the authority to reward or punish the consequences of that freedom at some future date. By the same token, the humans who bind themselves through the covenant limit their powers as well...." (68)

Wolfgang Roth and Rosemary Radford Ruether, *The Liberating Bond:*

- "A covenant relates the partners as whole persons (or communities) to each other and makes them (fictitious) sisters or brothers of each other. It is a flexible relationship where trust and faithfulness to each other determine the action of the partners." (2)

- "A covenant is a communion between partners, solemnly initiated, binding the partners into a new pattern of life and letting them mutually define each other. Covenant affects all aspects of the partners' lives, creating between and for them a sphere of interaction in loyalty to each other." (12)

• "A covenant is a more comprehensive and less legally defined relationship than a contract. A contract relates only to specific aspects of claims of human relationships; it seeks to regulate them according to a fixed standard. The covenant relates to persons as whole human beings; it humanizes interpersonal relationships." (13)

Sources Consulted

Balentine, Samuel E. *The Torah's Vision of Worship*. Minneapolis: Fortress Press, 1999.

Barton, William. *Congregational Creeds and Covenants*. Chicago: Advance Publishing Company, 1917.

Brueggemann, Walter. *The Covenanted Self: Explorations in Law and Covenant*. Minneapolis: Fortress Press, 1999.

———. *Old Testament Theology*. Minneapolis: Augsburg Fortress, 1997.

———. "The Risk of Heaven, the Possibility of Earth." Address to the Twelfth General Synod, 1979.

DeJong, Peter. *The Covenant Idea in New England Theology, 1620–1847*. Grand Rapids, Mich.: Wm. B. Eerdmans, 1945.

Elazar, Daniel. *Covenant and Polity in Biblical Israel*. Vol. 1 of *The Covenant Tradition in Politics*. New Brunswick, N.J.: Transaction Publishers, 1995.

Harrelson, Walter J. *The New Interpreter's Study Bible, New Revised Standard Version with Apocrypha*. Nashville: Abingdon Press, 2003.

Hartman, David. "The Theological Significance of Israel." Joseph Cardinal Bernardin Jerusalem Lecture. March 17, 1998.

Marty, Peter. "Breathing Together." *Christian Century* (August 23, 2005): 8–9.

Matthews, Victor. *Old Testament Themes*. St. Louis: Chalice Press, 2000

Rendle, Gilbert. *Behavioral Covenants in Congrega-
    tions: A Handbook for Honoring Differences* (Her-
    don, Va.: Alban Institute, 1998).

Roth, Wolfgang, and Rosemary Radford Ruether. *The
    Liberating Bond: Covenants — Biblical and Con-
    temporary.* New York: Friendship Press, 1978.

Sakenfeld, Katherine Doob. *New Interpreter's Dictio-
    nary of the Bible.* Nashville: Abingdon Press, 2007.

Walker, Randi. *The Evolution of a UCC Style: Essays in
    the History, Ecclesiology and Culture of the United
    Church of Christ.* Cleveland: United Church Press,
    2005.